AMISH SOCIETY